Secrets to a Successful Interview (bonus Q&A's)

Narmie Thambipillay
Career and Interview Confidence Coach

www.narmiet.com

Copyright © 2020 Narmatha Thambipillay

All rights reserved.

ISBN:

No part of this book may be reproduced, stored in a retrieval system or transmitted in any form. Reproduction by electronic, mechanical, photocopying, recording means or otherwise without prior written permission from the publisher, Narmie Thambipillay, is strictly forbidden.

The people and events described and depicted in this book are for educational purposes only. While every attempt has been made to verify information provided in this book, the author assumes no responsibility for any errors, inaccuracies or omissions.

The examples within this book are not intended to represent or guarantee that everyone or anyone will achieve their desired results. Each individual's success will be determined by his or her desire, dedication, effort and motivation. There are no guarantees you will achieve your desired outcome; the tools, stories and information are provided as examples only.

DEDICATION

To my beautiful son, Arjuna, who always has my back. He may be nine but his unwavering support and love for me really made it possible for me to get this book done. And to my mum and dad, without their immense support I would be lost!

I love you all!

CONTENTS

	Introduction	1
1	Various Stages of the Interview Process	3
2	Types of Interviews	6
3	References	17
4	Commonly Asked Questions	19
	Final Word	30
	About the Author	31

INTRODUCTION

You've got the call from the recruitment agent or the company saying, "Congrats – you have been successful in getting an interview."

But what should be music to your ears actually, fills you with fear.

How are you meant to dress? What could they ask? What should *you* be asking? Or more importantly, what are the things you *shouldn't* ask in the first interview? What if it's a phone interview or a panel interview? What do they mean when they say it's a 'behavioural' or 'competency-based' interview?

I remember going for my first interview and having no idea what to ask or how to answer certain questions. Nowadays, there's a lot more information on Google, but there's still nothing comprehensive and it's enough to send you into a world of overwhelm.

That's exactly why I wrote this book – it's a one-stop guide to the types of interviews that are out there and some practical questions for you to both practice answering and asking at the interviews.

I have purposely kept this book short and conversational to make sure you get all the important information without the stress. It's written in such a way that you don't have to read it chapter by chapter. Feel free to skip ahead to the chapter that is relevant to you.

At the end of this book, I've given you some of the commonly asked questions and potential answers to such questions you'll face in interviews.

It's my aim to help you walk into your interview with confidence, prepared for whatever they throw at you.

CHAPTER 1
VARIOUS STAGES OF THE INTERVIEW PROCESS

Believe it or not, interviews actually have stages. Most employers and recruiters will lay out the stages for you (especially for face-to-face interviews) but on the off-chance they don't, this chapter will help you get prepared for the unexpected.

The five common stages of an interview are:

1. Introduction
2. Questions by the interviewer
3. Questions by the interviewee
4. Closing
5. Follow-up

1. Introduction

In the introduction, the employer will introduce themselves and anyone else who happens to be in the interview with you. There will also be a bit of small talk on informal topics to gauge your personal interests.

2. Questions by the interviewer

This will be where most of your interview will be spent. We will go into more detail about specific questions later, but recruiters or employers will usually ask you open-ended questions and competency-based questions to test your skills and ability.

Some will also spend some time on your resume and going through your career (but hopefully this was already done in the initial phone interview). Remember, they want to know your background and whether what you have learnt in your previous roles and in your personal dealings will add value to their company.

Golden rule – if you don't understand the question, ask follow up questions or ask them to explain the question. The worst thing you can do is fudge and lie your way through a question.

3. Questions by the interviewee

This is where you get to ask the interviewer questions that you have previously prepared. In the past, "So what are the next steps?" was a frequently asked question and this was enough to satisfy the prospective employer that the potential candidate was interested. Sadly, this is no longer the case.

Remember, the interviewer may have already covered some of your questions during the interview stage, so be sure not to repeat yourself. However, if you feel like things weren't explained properly, be sure to ask for clarification.

Gain more insight into the position that may not have been covered. Ask open-ended questions to allow the employer to answer you fully. We'll cover some specific questions you can ask later in the book.

4. Closing

This is the part where you ask the employer what the next step in the hiring process is, including when you can expect to receive feedback on the interview and whether or not you have been successful. Remember to thank them for their time and always give a handshake.

5. Follow-up

Many people believe once they have walked out of the interview, that's it. However, you should always follow-up every interview with a quick email to thank the prospective employer for their time and reiterate your interest in the position.

CHAPTER 2
TYPES OF INTERVIEWS

Depending on the company and the type of role you are going for, you will invariably face one or many different types of interview formats. Below I have listed the different types of interviews you may face as well as ways to ensure you succeed so you get to the offer stage.

Coffee Interview

I wanted to quickly address this type of informal interview before I move on to the more formal types. Recruiters will often have "coffee meetings/interviews" with you to assess potential employment opportunities for you as opposed to when they are interviewing you for a specific role.

Things you should do:

- Prepare – the recruiter will give you some insight into why they want to talk to you, so make sure you know your CV inside out and be prepared to sell yourself with respect to your long-term goals and your next step.

- Ask lots of questions about the types of companies and roles they normally recruit for.
- Dress business casual (a suit would be over the top).

Things you should not do:

- Do not speak ill of your current workplace, colleagues, etc.
- Do not share names or personal details of colleagues or friends with the recruiter – even if they ask for referrals – without checking with the person first.

Questions to ask at the end:

- What was the purpose of this meeting?
- Can you tell me a bit about any of the roles you believe may be suitable for me?
- What's next from here?
- What's the best way to keep in contact?

We'll now move onto the more formal interviews – by this I mean where you're interviewing for a particular role that you have either applied for or been headhunted for.

Phone Interview

There are two types of phone interviews:

6. When you are caught off guard by the recruiter (it's usually just a fact-finding mission by the recruiter, or an 'initial chat' as its sometimes called).

7. When you've had time to prepare and they call you back at a specific time.

Let's discuss the 'unprepared' one first. Usually, these calls will take you off guard as you are busy going about your day. Because of this, it's easy to come off sounding nervous, hesitant or just plain distracted.

If you're not actually able to talk or don't feel comfortable having the "initial chat" at that time, tell the person that. It's better to be honest and reschedule to a more appropriate time than trying to wing it and end up messing it up.

These initial chats can either be a full-blown interview or just a fact-finding mission to gauge your interest in the job. They usually want to find out whether you're a potential good fit for the role. These initial chats are also used as screening calls in case there are a few different candidates they cannot distinguish between.

Now let's talk about the interviews you've had time to prepare for.

The key to a scheduled phone interview is to ensure you're in a quiet area with no background noise or distractions.

Things you should do:

- Have a fully charged phone (it sounds simple enough, but you would be surprised how many people forget).
- Go somewhere quiet and away from distractions.
- Make sure you speak clearly into the phone.
- Ask the recruiter to repeat a question if you don't understand them fully.

Things you should not do:

- Use speakerphone – if you need to write notes or don't want to hold your phone, use earphones. With a speakerphone, the interviewer may not be able to hear or may miss certain things you say (this could be the difference between getting to the next round or not).

- Multi-task – you should treat phone interviews like face-to-face interviews. No drinking your cup of coffee or finishing off your dinner while talking.
- Elaborate on your answers too much – unlike in a face-to-face interview, you cannot read the interviewer's body language, so you don't know if they are still listening or have tuned out. My advice is to keep your answers short and to the point. If they need to, they will ask you to expand on your answers.

Questions to ask at the end:

- Can you give me more information about the responsibilities of this role?
- Why has this role come up?
- When are you expecting someone to start?
- What are the next steps?
- When can I expect feedback?

Sometimes the first interview can be a video interview instead of a phone interview. In this case, what should you do differently?

Video Interview

The key here is to be prepared. Do a test-run beforehand on Skype or whatever program you're using to ensure it's working, that your login details are correct, etc. Nothing can fluster you faster than when the technology doesn't work. Try and log in at least five minutes prior to the interview to reduce stress.

Things you should do:

- Ensure your background is tidy – or better yet, facing a blank white wall.

- Check the lighting where you will be doing the video conference – the interviewer wants to be able to see you clearly.
- Dress the way you would if you were attending a face-face interview (i.e. professionally).
- During the interview, turn off your phone, TV, and anything else that could potentially distract you.
- Maintain eye contact and make sure you talk to the interviewer (this means looking through the camera lens when answering questions, not looking at yourself on the screen).

Things you should not do:

- Tap a pen, your foot, etc. – the mic will pick this up and it can be very distracting for the interviewer.
- Act too casual – remember, a video interview should be treated exactly the same as a face-to-face interview.
- Read things off your computer screen – if you want to have notes, have a pen and paper next to you.
- Have your phone close to you as it could distract you.

Commonly Asked Questions:

- Tell me about your current role?
- Why are you looking to leave?
- What are your salary expectations?
- What are you looking for in your new role?
- What is it you are not willing to compromise on?
- Which of your requirements are negotiable (nice to haves)?
- What is it about this job ad that appealed to you? (If you don't remember the ad, be honest about it).

Questions to ask at the end:

- Can you give me more information about the responsibilities of this role?
- Why has this role come up?
- When are you expecting someone to start?
- What are the next steps?
- When can I expect feedback?

Face-to-Face Interview

Congratulations on making it past the initial phone interview! The face-to-face interview can be quite daunting as you're meeting your prospective employer for the first time. It all counts, from your interaction with the receptionist through to the very end when you shake hands to say goodbye.

So, let's start with how you should dress. Even if the company you are interviewing for has a casual dress style, my recommendation for men is to wear a suit (tie is optional depending on how corporate the environment is); women should opt for a corporate dress and jacket, or a corporate skirt or pants and jacket.

Things you should do:

- Turn up at least five minutes early. Of course, things happen – if you're going to be late, make sure you call and let them know approximately how late you think you'll be.
- Turn your phone off or put it on silent.
- Always greet the receptionist in a friendly manner.
- Greet your interviewer with a firm handshake.
- Get the interviewer's business card.
- Maintain eye contact with your interviewer.
- Speak clearly and, once again, if you don't understand a question, ask the interviewer to repeat the question.

- Thank the interviewer for their time and express interest in the role.

Things you should not do:

- Smoke prior to the interview.
- Lie or make up answers to questions – if you genuinely don't have the experience or it's not relevant, it's better to be upfront.
- Say anything negative about your current role or colleagues – it really doesn't leave a good impression in the interviewer's mind.
- Answer questions with "yes" or "no" – always elaborate with examples.
- Discuss personal or family issues.
- If it's an interview with the potential employer and not a recruiter, do not inquire about the salary or additional benefits.

Commonly Asked Questions:

- Tell me about your current role?
- Why are you looking to leave?
- What are your salary expectations?
- What are you looking for in your new role?
- What is it you are not willing to compromise on?

Questions to ask at the end:
- Do you need any clarification on anything I have answered?
- What are the next steps?
- What gets rewarded at this company? (This question will give you an insight into the company culture).

Make sure you send a follow-up thank you email to the interviewer expressing your interest in the role and thanking them for their time. If you got the interview through a recruiter, be sure to contact them immediately and give them feedback on what you liked, did not like, and anything you want further clarification on.

Well done! You have made it past the initial interview (either with the recruiter or the employer). If your second interview is with the employer, refer to the first interview do's and don'ts. If your second interview is now with someone else in your potential place of employment, see below.

To be honest, there really isn't much difference between the first interview with the employer and the second, except the second may be more behavioural-based.

Panel Interview

Unlike the one-on-one face interview, panel interviews are a lot more structured. The panel usually consists of HR, a line manager, and maybe a few others you may report to or other team members.

Things you should do:

- Introduce yourself and shake hands with everyone on the panel.
- Ask for business cards from each of them.
- Look at the person who asks you the question and try to look at each of the panel members when you are answering.
- Speak clearly, and once again, if you don't understand the question, ask them to clarify.
- Thank the interviewers for their time and express your interest in the role.

Things you should not do:

- Lie or make up answers to questions – if you genuinely don't have the experience or it's not relevant, it's better to be up front.
- Say anything negative about your current role, colleagues etc. – it really doesn't leave a good impression in the interviewers' minds.
- Inquire about the salary or additional benefits.
- Answer questions with "yes" or "no" – always elaborate with examples.
- Discuss personal or family issues.

Commonly asked behavioural-based questions:

- Tell me about your current role.
- Describe a situation where you had to deal with a difficult team member and how you handled it.
- Tell me about your strengths.
- What do you consider your weakness?

Questions to ask at the end:

- Do you need any clarification on anything I have answered?
- What are the next steps?
- What gets rewarded at this company? (This question will give you an insight into the company culture).

Don't forget to send a follow-up email to the panel after your interview thanking them for their time. You can send one email addressing all the interviewers.

Team-based interview

As culture and teamwork are important in the workplace nowadays, a lot of employers will do some kind of team-based meeting. If that means drinks at their local hangout, do not be complacent. It's still an interview, just in a relaxed environment.

You should be quietly confident because it basically means if you click with the team you have the job. However, you may not be the only person being interviewed, so what should you do and what should you *not* do?

Things you should do:

- Be on your best interview behaviour. Leave your usual 'Friday night with the friends' attitude at home.
- Open up and enjoy yourself.

Things you should not do:

- Get drunk.
- Be too formal.

Questions to ask at the end:

- What's the team culture?
- What is the company culture? (It's always good to get their perspective).
- How long have you been with the company?
- What do you enjoy about your role?

Remember, although this is an informal setting, it's usually the last step before being offered the job. So, while you should have fun, don't go overboard. Also, make sure you're assessing whether you can see yourself as part of this team.

Finally – I've mentioned this above but I'm going to reiterate – please make sure you send a follow-up email thanking the interviewers for their time, stating your interest in the job. This is also a good opportunity to get further clarification on anything you're unsure about.

CHAPTER 3
REFERENCES

Congratulations! You made it through the grueling interview process and you are now at the reference stage.

So, who should your referee be? Ideally, your last two managers or someone you reported to. However, sometimes this might not be ideal. Perhaps you and your manager didn't get along and you're worried they could jeopardise your chance of success.

DO NOT get one of your friends to act as a fake manager. Eventually you will get found out as some employers will call the reception of your current workplace to see if that person actually works there.

So, what *should* you do? Be upfront with your prospective employer and find out who else they would be willing to accept as a referee. Most of the time, they will be happy to accept a fellow colleague or even another manager whom you may have worked with previously.

If your manager is no longer working with the company and you have no idea how to get in touch with them, let the prospective employer know and they will come up with an alternative suggestion.

ALWAYS double check before you put someone down as a referee. Some people are either not comfortable being one or, more importantly, the company may not allow people to give references.

Finally, even if someone knows they are a referee, it's a good idea to give them a heads up to expect a phone call and just a brief rundown of your roles and responsibilities so your reference can be well prepared when the call comes through.

For your own peace of mind, it's always nice to check in with your referee later, not just to thank them for their time but also so you know how the reference check went.

CHAPTER 4
COMMONLY ASKED QUESTIONS

The following questions are just a sample of the many potential questions you could be asked. However, during my time as a recruiter, I've found these to be the most commonly asked (or some variation of these). If you can prepare answers to these questions, you'll be ahead of the game.

"Tell me about yourself."

This is a great time for you to tell them what you would like them to know about you. Remember, an interview is about *selling* yourself. Prepare three to five key points about yourself that you would like them to know.

Example 1:

A candidate of mine was going for a role as a Physiotherapist within the Aged Care Sector. Her answer to this was: "I am a passionate physiotherapist who enjoys working with the elderly as I enjoy that continuity of care that comes with this role. It also enables me to get to know my patient in a personal manner as well as a professional manner."

Example 2:

A candidate of mine who worked as a legal secretary said: "One of the things I thoroughly enjoy is working with a manager who allows me autonomy and flexibility with work. I love getting to work with a number of managers as that keeps me busy and challenged."

"Why are you looking to leave?"

NEVER badmouth your previous employer – even if that's the reason you are looking to leave. Instead, use the job description as a basis for your answer.

Example:

My candidate, the legal secretary, answered: "I believe this role will be more of a challenge as this is a much bigger firm and so the cases will be more complex. I'm also looking forward to working with multiple reports as opposed to just the two I'm reporting to now."

"Why did you leave your previous role?"

This is easy if you jumped from one role to the other – just say that you left for a better opportunity. If you were made redundant, that should already be on your CV, but it doesn't hurt to reiterate. If you were fired, there is no need to let them know this either.

Example:

"In hindsight, I probably wasn't the best fit for the role and despite achieving (*talk about things that are similar to the role you are interviewing for*), I wasn't very strong in other parts of the role so I decided it was time to go my own way."

What if you have been unemployed for some time? As I said above, never bad mouth your previous company.

Example:

"There really was no scope for me to grow in my previous role even though I had achieved x,y,z, and so I gave my notice to my employer, ensured there was a handover with the person who took over – after all, I didn't want to leave my employer high and dry – and then left."

"Can you explain this gap in your work history?"

As mentioned previously, this should already be addressed in your CV, however, employers like to hear from you to see if it's something that could reoccur. If it was due to being let go, use the previous example. If it was something else like maternity leave, illness, etc. just be honest.

Example:

"I have been looking for work, however during this time I have – *discuss any activities, studies, etc. you may have done to build on your skills.*"

"What are you looking for in your new role?"

Your answer to this should be built around the job description and things that will motivate you on a day-to-day basis. You can throw in that after researching the company, you would be keen to work for them because of x, y, z.

Example:

A candidate of mine was going for a Relationship Manager role with a German Bank. Her answer was: "Dealing with people on a daily basis is something that I thoroughly enjoy as can be seen in my previous roles. However, what excites me most about this role is getting to work for yourselves because I learnt German in school and ever since then I've always wanted to work for you." (NB. There is nothing wrong with being authentic and truthful about such things).

"What type of environment do you like to work in?"

With this question, they are trying to work out whether you are going to be compatible with their environment. Focus on things like working in a team environment – one where you can collaborate with your team and help each other out when the need arises.

"Where do you see yourself in five years' time?"

While this is such an outdated question, there are still a number of firms that like to ask it. A great way to address this is: "I would ideally like to stay in this role for at least the next 18-24 months as I believe it will take me that long to learn everything I need to about this particular role. After that (if the opportunity doesn't arise beforehand), I would like to take on more responsibility and naturally look at career progression within the company."

"What would you say is a weakness of yours?"

This is a common question and one where a lot of candidates tend to stumble, so make sure you prepare this answer thoroughly. Your answer should be something that can also be seen as a strength.

Example:

The candidate going for the relationship manager role answered: "As you can tell I enjoy the relationship side of my role a lot but sometimes I can spend more time with a client or a colleague than is probably necessary. However, I guess the positive of it is that I have great relationships with my clients and colleagues."

"What would you say are your strengths?"

This is a common question and usually goes hand-in-hand with the previous question about weaknesses. Think about what you can bring to this role.

Example 1:

The relationship manager said her greatest strength was verbal communication and the ability to empathise with others.

Example 2:

The Physiotherapist said her greatest strength was her friendly personality and her ability to think outside the box.

"How soon can you start?"

If you are currently employed, let them know what your current notice period is, whether that be two or four weeks. Sometimes, they will push you to start earlier by saying they ideally want someone to start sooner than that.

The best way of handling this is to say: "I totally understand that, however, I would like to do the right thing by my current employer and give them time to find my replacement so as not to leave them high and dry. I do, however, have annual leave left so I may be able to use that against my notice period, but I won't know this until receiving my offer letter."

What's good about the above answer is that it shows your prospective employer that even though you are looking to leave you are still loyal and you want to do the right thing. This will make you stand out as the type of person everyone wants to hire.

"What are your salary expectations?"

This is a simple question but one that tends to trip up a lot of my candidates. If you give too low a salary it can sometimes reflect badly upon you as it gets the manager wondering why you are pricing yourself too low.

On the flipside, if you price yourself too high, it will leave them wondering why you would ever accept a job which involves a pay drop and your subsequent commitment to the role.

Make sure you research your role on various job sites and talk to your recruitment agent (if you used one) on what they would suggest.

The best way to answer this is: "Prior to me answering that, can you advise me on how much you have budgeted for this role?"

Then simply say: "That actually ties in with the range I was looking for."

What if they won't give you a range? Since you have done your research, you can say: "I've done some research on these types of roles and based on my previous experience and what I can offer to you, I'm looking for anything between X and Y, however I am open to discussion should I be the right candidate for this role."

"Are you interviewing anywhere else that we need to be aware

of?"

They could be asking this for two reasons. One is to see how quickly they need to move with respect to getting you an offer. On the other hand, if you have been unemployed for quite some time and don't have anything in the pipeline, companies can get wary about being the first one to give you a chance.

The best way to answer this question is to say: "I've had a couple of interviews I am waiting to hear back from, and another couple this week and next, however nothing is set in stone yet."

BEHAVIOURAL-BASED QUESTIONS

Behavioural-based questions are quite common nowadays and are used as a way for the prospective employer to ascertain how you would behave in certain situations. Naturally, the examples you use to back up these questions should be work-based. However, if you're unable to relate it to anything at work, then for sure use personal examples.

If you're still unable to think of anything that would relate, be honest and say: "Unfortunately, I really cannot think of any situation I have been in where this has occurred, however, if I was ever in that situation, I believe I would…" This lets the interviewer know you are being honest, but still gives them an insight into how you might approach such a situation.

"Tell me a time you made a mistake at work and what happened."

We've all made mistakes, whether it's a major or minor one. What the interviewer is trying to see here is whether you can be open and honest. By understanding the process, you took to rectify the situation, they also get an insight into your problem-solving ability.

Example:

"We had a major project due for a client and each of us in the team were responsible for certain aspects of it. However, more than once a team member did not come to the meetings as required. The problem is that when it came time for final submission, this team member was not ready and that meant we ended up having to delay the launch date which upset the client. We ended up having to put in a lot of extra hours to make sure the delay wasn't too extensive. What I realised from this is the need to keep on top of all team members and to ensure that everyone is held accountable. I have not made that mistake again."

"Tell me about a difficult situation at work and how you handled it."

While it's good to be honest in all situations, make sure you avoid situations where you are the cause of the issue.

Example:

"As a relationship manager, I was the middle person between my team and the client. Unfortunately, there was a situation whereby my team had missed a particular thing on one of the trades. This made the client quite upset and what made it worse was the team member kept trying to hide behind his mistake and blame the client. I had to be sure to remain neutral and undertake the necessary investigations to see what had happened. We ended up resolving the issue with the trade and I apologised to the client for the delay and that it was an oversight which going forward I would ensure would not happen. With my team member, I had a chat with them about pulling together as a team and that we all make mistakes but at least if he was honest, we could have fixed the situation before it escalated. From this situation, I put into place measures to ensure daily, as well as weekly, reporting and consolidation of outstanding trades, so this situation never occurred again."

As you can see from the above example, the relationship manager gave a brief explanation of the difficult situation, but then mentioned the steps she put in place to not just handle the situation but also to ensure it wouldn't occur again. Also, note she never blamed anyone – it was purely factual.

"Give me an example of a time you had to deal with an angry client or customer."

If you have not dealt with an angry client or customer, you could also discuss a time you had a misunderstanding with a colleague.

Example:

The relationship manager drew on the difficult situation example: "As I mentioned with the trade being missed, my client was really angry with myself and my team. I made sure I jumped on a phone call with them to try and calm the situation as they were wanting to escalate things to my manager. I also made sure I listened to what the client had to say and gave them time to vent. I asked her to please give me a few days to work out what had happened and to rectify the situation. Lucky for me, based on our relationship, they gave me the required time and we were able to fix the issue. During this process, I made sure I kept my client in the loop the entire way via email – just so they knew that we were working on it.

After being able to rectify the situation, I once again jumped on a call to let them what had happened on our end and to let them know this would not happen again. My client thanked me for my professionalism and for taking charge to make things right. They also sent a follow-up email to my manager to let them know that I had gone - what they believed was - above and beyond to ensure our relationship became stronger."

"Tell me a time you went above and beyond the scope of your role."

This is a great time for you to highlight your strengths and really sell yourself.

Example:

The legal secretary drew on this example: "One of the things I love is working in a team environment. One of the secretaries in the other team was run off her feet as a couple of her direct reports had a legal matter to be heard in court. Unfortunately, this meant that she was not able to look after the lawyer. Since I was not as busy, and after checking with my manager to make sure they were ok with this, I offered to look after the requirements of that lawyer until such time as things had settled down for the secretary. She was highly appreciative as was the lawyer who was being impacted."

"Tell me about a time you had a disagreement with your manager."

At one time or another, we've all disagreed with our managers, whether it be because they are unaware of everything that is going on, or they may see a different way to solve a problem. What the interviewer is looking for is to make sure you and your manager listened to each other's point of views and that you were able to resolve the issue amicably, even if that meant the argument didn't end in your favour.

"Tell me about a time you had to work with someone you did not get along with."

This is a tricky question as it involves talking negatively about someone else – which as I have mentioned before, you should never do. The best way to answer this question is to remain neutral about the situation.

Example:

The relationship manager said: "Every Monday, all members of my team were required to submit a report of outstanding trades. However, on a consistent basis one of my team would not get this to me till the next day or even a couple of days later which was quite frustrating. As this was starting to have a flow-on effect, I had to have a conversation with her which unfortunately involved me having to put her on performance management. Anyway, after a couple of weeks things did improve and she started submitting the reports on time; however she did leave shortly afterwards as she felt the role was not for her."

These are just a few examples of some of the questions you may be asked and ways to answer them. Ensure that you tailor your responses to suit your CV and situations that you have been in.

Key point: Do not lie or make things up – it will come out some way.

Be prepared and you will be well on your way to succeeding in your next job interview!

FINAL WORD

This book has been done to be your go to book on interviews. I hope you found it helpful and it gave you an insight into what to expect at the various interview stages. I sincerely wish you the very best of luck in your next job interview and hope this book helps you nail it!

If you need more help with your interviews or have any questions, check out www.narmiet.com and leave us a comment. On the website, you'll find helpful videos on how to answer some of the questions we've covered as well.

ABOUT THE AUTHOR

Narmie Thambipillay has been in recruitment for over 10 years. During this time, she has interviewed and successfully helped hundreds of candidates secure their dream job, some even their first job since moving countries or graduating university.

Through conducting 1000's of interviews during her time as a recruitment expert, Narmie came to realise that candidates are afraid of interviews and are looking for that extra edge over their competition, but there was little information available to help people through the process with confidence. Hence she wrote this book.

Narmie is the founder of Narmiet– a company dedicated to help professionals and graduates to overcome their fear during the interview process.

Her office is located in Australia but she has helped clients all over the world nail their interviews with confidence.

To find out more about how Narmie can help you, visit her narmiet.com/contact

Secrets to a Successful Interview

www.ingramcontent.com/pod-product-compliance
Lightning Source LLC
Chambersburg PA
CBHW070906220526
45466CB00005B/2149